SWU-NAP- 021

UNIFORMS OF RUSSIAN ARMY DURING THE NAPOLEONIC WAR VOL.16

UNDER THE REIGN OF ALEXANDER I
EMPEROR OF RUSSIA BETWEEN 1801 AND 1825
GUARDS CAVALRY: CUIRASSIERS, DRAGOONS & OTHERS

From the Viskovatov's greatest work:
"Historical description of the clothing and
arms of the Russian Army"

English translation by Mark Conrad

SOLDIERSHOP PUBLISHING

AUTHOR

Aleksandr Vasilevich Viskovatov born 22 April (4 May New Style) 1804, died 27 February (11 March) 1858 in St. Petersburg, Russian military historian. He graduated from the 1st Cadet Corps and served in the artillery, the hydrographic depot of the Naval Ministry, and then in the Department of Military Educational Institutions. He mainly studied historical artifacts and the histories of military units. Viskovatov's greatest work was the Historical Description of the Clothing and Arms of the Russian Army.

PUBLISHING'S NOTE

None of **unpublished** images or text of our book may be reproduced in any format without the expressed written permission of Soldiershop.com when not indicate as marked with license creative commons 3.0 or 4.0. The publisher remains to disposition of the possible having right for all the doubtful sources images or not identifies. Our trademark: Soldiershop Publishing ©, The names of our series: Soldiers&Weapons, Battlefield, War in colour, PaperSoldiers, Soldiershop e-book etc. are herein © by Soldiershop.com.

NOTE ABOUT BOOK PRINTING BEFORE 1925

This book may contain text or images coming from a reproduction of a book published before 1925 (over seventy years ago). No effort has been made to modernize or standardize the spelling used in the original text, so this book may have occasional imperfections such as missing or blurred pages, poor pictures, errant marks, etc. that were either part of the original artifact, or were introduced by the scanning process. We believe this work is culturally important, and despite the imperfections, have elected to bring it back into print (digital and/or paper) as part of our continuing commitment to the preservation of printed works worldwide. We appreciate your understanding of the imperfections in the preservation process, and hope you enjoy this valuable book. Now this book is purpose re-built and is proof-read and re-type set from the original to provide an outstanding experience of reflowing text, also for an ebook reader. However Soldiershop publishing added, enriched, revised and overhauled the text, images, etc. of the cover and the book. Therefore, the job is now to all intents and purposes a derivative work, and the added, new and original parts of the book are the copyright of Soldiershop. On this second unpublished part of the book none of images or text may be reproduced in any format without the expressed written permission of Soldiershop. Almost many of the images of our books and prints are taken from original first edition prints or books that are no longer in copyright and are therefore public domain. We have been a specialized bookstore for a long time so we (and several friends antiquarian booksellers) have readily available a lot of ancient, historical and illustrated books not in copyright. Each of our prints, art designs or illustrations is either our own creation, or a fully digitally restoration by our computer artists, or non copyrighted images. All of our prints are "tagged" with a registered digital copyright. Soldiershop remains to disposition of the possible having right for all the doubtful sources images or not identifies.

LICENSES COMMONS

Much of the text in this book are from the *"Memoirs of the Empress Catherine II., by Catherine II, Empress of Russia"* This book is for the use of anyone anywhere at no cost and with almost no restrictions whatsoever. You may copy it, give it away or re-use it under the terms of the similar creative commons License. This book may utilize material marked with license creative commons 3.0 or 4.0 (CC BY 4.0), (CC BY-ND 4.0), (CC BY-SA 4.0) or (CC0 1.0). We give appropriate attribution credit and indicate if change were made below in the acknowledgements field.

ACKNOWLEDGEMENTS

A Special Thanks to NYPL and other institutions for their kindly permission to use some images of his archives, collections or books used in our book.

Title: **UNIFORMS OF RUSSIAN ARMY DURING THE NAPOLEONIC WAR VOL. 16**
The Guards Cavalry: Cuirassiers, Dragoons & Others
By A.V.Viskovatov. Serie edit by Luca S. Cristini. First edition by Soldiershop. March 2018
Cover & Art Design: Luca S. Cristini. Plates re-colorations by Anna Cristini.
ISBN code: 978-88-93273091
Published by Soldiershop publishing, via Padre Davide, 7 - 24050 Zanica (BG) ITALY. www.soldiershop.com

UNIFORMS OF THE RUSSIAN ARMY DURING THE NAPOLEONIC WAR VOL. 16

UNDER THE REIGN OF ALEXANDER I EMPEROR OF RUSSIA BETWEEN 1801 AND 1825

*

THE GUARDS CAVALRY: CUIRASSIERS, DRAGOONS & OTHERS

Russland.

Rgt. Moskau. Rgt. Borissoglebsk. Rgt. Kargopol
Rgt. Kurland. Rgt. Kinburn Offizier.
Unteroffizier.

Dragoner.

1813.

Die Dragoner trugen Koletts wie die Infanterie, vorn mit 2 Reihen von je 6 Knöpfen. Die Schossaumschläge waren, unabhängig von der Abzeichenfarbe, durchweg rot. In die beiden Taillenknöpfe wurden Tuchtaschen eingeknöpft, um dem Leibkoppel festeren Sitz zu geben. 1814 erlitt die Uniform einige Aenderungen. Die Koletts erhielten nunmehr eine Reihe von 9 Knöpfen. Die Beinkleider wurden mit einem Seitenvorstoss zwischen zwei Tuchstreifen geschmückt, die die Abzeichenfarbe des Regiments zeigten. Dazu wurden Karabiner eingeführt. 1817 schaffte man den Helm ab und ersetzte ihn durch einen hohen Czako. Die Offiziere erhielten Kartuschen mit Bandelier.

HISTORICAL DESCRIPTION OF THE CLOTHING AND ARMS
OF THE RUSSIAN ARMY - A.V. VISKOVATOV
(First English translation by Mark Conrad)

Soldiershop is glad to presents the complete collection of the great job made by A.V. Viskovatov dedicated to the uniforms and weapons belonging to the Russian army during the Napoleonic period, until 1825. The time we considered corresponds to the reigns of two Tzars: Paul I, who reigned since 1769 until his murder on the 23rd of March 1801, and his son Aleksandr Pavlovič Romanov, that with the title of Alexander I, sat on the throne until the 1st December 1825.

Our reprint in based on the original 19th century volumes, to be precise the volumes from 7 to 9 are dedicated to the reign of Paul I; this first part is distributed on 7 volumes, having a numbering from 1 to 7. From number 10 to 18 of the original volumes, the second part is dedicated to the Russian troops under Alexander I. These still being worked on and they will be soon ready, distributed on twenty volumes approximately. Our new edition, the first ever published in English, both on paper and digital format, boasts a large number of color plates, many of them unpublished and coloured by our team of expert artists and scholars of uniformology. Each volume is based on 50/70 plates, always accompanied by the original translated text which describes the uniforms, the organization and the armament of the Russian army of the period.

In this book we present the Russian Guards cavalry regiments of the Napoleonic wars (1st part).

A unique work in its genre, a must have in any respecting collection!

Aleksandr Vasilevich Viskovatov born 22 April (4 May New Style) 1804, died 27 February (11 March) 1858 in St. Petersburg, Russian military historian. He graduated from the 1st Cadet Corps and served in the artillery, the hydrographic depot of the Naval Ministry, and then in the Department of Military Educational Institutions.

He mainly studied historical artifacts and the histories of military units. Viskovatov's greatest work was the Historical Description of the Clothing and Arms of the Russian Army (Vols. 1-30, St. Petersburg, 1841-62; 2nd ed. Vols. 1-34, St. Petersburg - Novosibirsk - Leningrad, 1899-1948). This work is based on a great quantity of archival documents and contains four thousand colored illustrations.

Viskovatov was the author of Chronicles of the Russian Army (Books 1-20, St. Petersburg, 1834-42) and Chronicles of the Russian Imperial Army (Parts 1-7, St. Petersburg, 1852). He collected valuable material on the history of the Russian navy which went into A Short Overview of Russian Naval Campaigns and General Voyages to the End of the XVII Century (St. Petersburg, 1864; 2nd edition Moscow, 1946). Together with A.I. Mikhailovskii-Danilevskii he helped prepare and create the Military Gallery in the Winter Palace.

He wrote the historical military inscriptions for the walls of the Hall of St. George in the Great Palace of the Kremlin. (From the article in the Soviet Military Encyclopedia.)

CONTENTS

*

Preface pag. 5

*

Guards Cuirassiers pag. 7

Guards Dragoons pag. 13

Guards Horse-Jaegers pag. 15

Notes. pag. 18

*

PLATES pag. 21

RUSSIAN ARMY- GUARDS CAVALRY
CHANGES IN THE UNIFORMS AND EQUIPMENT OF GUARDS CAVALRY FROM 1801 TO 1825.

XXXIII. GUARDS CUIRASSIERS.
[Gvardeiskie kirasiry.]

9 April 1801 - Lower ranks of the Cavalier Guards and L.-Gds. Horse Regiments were ordered to cut off their **curls** [*pukli*] and have **queues** [*kosy*] only 4 vershoks [7 inches] long, tying them midway down the collar [1].

17 July 1801 – Cavalier Guards non-commissioned officers were ordered to have **pouches** [*lyadunki*] to hold pistol cartridges instead of—as was the previous practice—having nest-like spaces [*gnezdy*] in the holsters. [2].

21 July 1801 – Generals and field and company-grade officers of the Cavalier Guards and L.-Gds. Horse Regiments were given **hats** of a new pattern, completely identical to those introduced in 1802 in Army Cuirassier regiments, and already described above [3].

9 August 1801 - The **cuirasses** [*kirasy*] in both regiments were withdrawn [4].

27 February 1802 — Officers of both regiments were ordered to have short **gloves** without gauntlets, of the pattern used at this time by infantry officers [5].

17 March 1802 — The regulations confirmed on this date regarding the cut, trim, and pattern of **cuirassier uniforms**, for combatant as well as for noncombatant ranks, were also adopted for the Cavalier Guards and L.-Gds. Horse Regiments. Based on these and on special models confirmed by HIGHEST Authority, *private* Cavalier Guardsmen had the following clothing, accouterments, weapons, and horse furniture:

Coat [kolet] – single breasted, of white cloth, with two cloth shoulder straps; standing collar, slit cuffs, piping at the shoulder seams of the sleeves and on the shoulder straps and skirt turnbacks—of crimson cloth; cloth piping, also crimson, along both sides of the coat's front opening, on which was sewn silver galloon; two silver galloon buttonhole loops on the cuffs; white cloth lining and piping along the upper and side edges of the collar; tinned brass buttons of which one was prescribed to be on each shoulder strap, one at the bottom of each skirt, and two at the waist; the coat's front opening was closed with small hooks (Illus. 1987).

Hat [shlyapa] – with swhite worsted buttonhole loop, similar to the silver loop for officers, and with small red tassels (Illus. 1987).

Girdle [kushak] – of crimson serge (Illus. 1987).

Sabertache [tashka] – of crimson cloth, with toothed silver galloon at the edges; silver embroidered star in the center, of the same form as on Guards officers' shabracks, and with red Russian leather straps (Illus. 1987).

Broadsword [palash] – of the previous pattern as used under EMPEROR PAUL I, i.e. with a silvered hilt with a two-headed eagle, and a black leather scabbard with a slit iron frame (Illus. 1987).

Swordknot and sword belt [temlyak i portupeya] – of red Russian leather (Illus. 1987).

Crossbelt (for the carbine) and pouch belt [pogonnaya (k karabinu) i lyadunochnaya perevyazi] – white (deerskin), trimmed at the edges with narrow silver galloon with crimson cloth piping, and worn crosswise over each other (Illus. 1987).

Pouch [lyadunka] – of black leather, of the standard cuirassier pattern for that time; with the same star on the lid as was on the sabertache but of forged and stamped metal instead of embroidered.

Shabrack and pistol carriers [cheprak i chushki] – of crimson cloth with a single row of silver galloon, and the same stars as on the sabertache (Illus. 1987).

Greatcoat [shinel'] – of gray cloth, with a standing collar and two shoulder straps of black cloth; the same buttons as on the *kolet* coat (Illus. 1987).

Forage cap [furazhnaya shapka] – of white cloth, with a black cloth band and red cloth piping between the seams; a white and crimson tassel with a slide [*gaika*] according to the squadron: in the 1st—white, in the 2nd—sky blue, in the 3rd—yellow (Illus. 1987).

All other items were prescribed to be the same, and of the same patterns, as for the Army Cuirrasier regiments described above [6].

Non-commissioned officers – had silver galloon on the coat collar and cuffs (Illus. 1988), while *trumpeters* had swallows' nests at the shoulders, in the same color as the collar, and sewn-on silver galloon stripes. In other respects distinctions of these ranks from private Cavalier Guardsmen were the same as in Army Cuirassier regiments [7].

Officers – had uniform clothing of the same colors and patterns as for private Cavalier Guardsmen, but without piping at the shoulder seams; a silver galloon shoulder strap on the left shoulder; straight-sided silver galloon, piped in red cloth down its edges, at the coat's front opening and on the pouch belt; the same broadsword hilt as for lower ranks, with that sword being worn in a frog. Shabracks and pistol carriers werer trimmed with toothed silver galloon. All else was prescribed to be the same as for officers of HIS MAJESTY's Leib-Cuirassier Regiment (Illus. 1989 and 1990) [8].

29 December 1802 – Confirmation was given to a table of uniforms, accouterments, and arms for the **L.-Gds. Horse Regiment**, based on which it was given the same uniforms, weaponry, and horse furniture as received in this year by

HIS MAJESTY's Leib-Cuirassier Regiment, but with a crimson collar and cuffs, sewn-on lace or buttonhole loops after pattern used in the L.-Gds. Preobrazhenskii Regiment, crimson piping and collar tabs on the greatcoat, copper ("red brass") buttons and other metal appointments—but gilt for officers, gold galloon (including on the pouch belt), dark-blue shabracks and pistol carriers that for lower ranks are trimmed with red tape decorated with yellow tracery. A further difference was that for Army Cuirassiers the carbine hook was on the pouch belt, but in the L.-Gds. Horse Regiment the hook and the pouch had their own belts worn crosswise, as related above for the Cavalier Guards. Officers wore an aiguilette on the right shoulder (Illus. 1991, 1992, 1993, and 1994) [9]. Kettledrum banners were of crimson velvet with gold (Illus. 1995) [10], while the kettledrums and trumpets themselves, from the founding of the regiment, remained silver.

Like Army Cuirassier officers, the officers of the L.-Gds. Horse Regiment had an *undress coat and frock coat [vitse-mundir i sertuk]*, of which the first was referred to as the *red undress coat* and the second as the *dark-green undress coat*.

The *red undress coat* for officers of the L.-Gds. Horse Regiment was of the same pattern as established in 1802 for the white cuirassier undress coat but in red, with dark-blue collar, cuffs, skirttail lining, and turnbacks, and with gold embroidered but-

Russian Cuirassier Regiments in 1814 by Knotel

tonhole loops on the collar and cuffs (Illus. 1996). The *frock coat* or *dark-green undress coat* was also of Army Cuirassier pattern, but with red piping and gold buttons (Illus. 1997). The *shabrack* and *pistol carriers* for use with both undress coats were prescribed to be of the same patterns as used with white Cuirassier undress coats, in dark blue with gold embroidery (Illus. 1997) [11].

13 February 1803 – The silver buttonhole loops on the **cuffs** of lower ranks in the Cavalier Guards Regiment were removed, and instead they were ordered to have two buttons on each cuff. These buttons were the same as on the shoulder straps. The decorative tracery buttonhole loop on the **hat** was replaced with narrow straight-sided lace, without any toothed pattern (Illus. 1998) [12].

18 October 1803 – When in formation, all combatant ranks of the Cavalier Guards and L.-Gds. Horse Regiment were ordered to wear **helmets** with thick hair plumage. These were the same as introduced at this same time for Army Cuirassiers, Dragoons, and Horse Artillery, but with copper ("red brass") fittings and with a star in front instead of an eagle. For lower ranks the star was of stamped out of the brass while for officers it was silver and separately attached, with enamel on the rim of the circle and in the circle itself (Illus. 1999, 2000, and 2001) [13].

6 November 1803 – The **Cavalier Guards Regiment** was ordered to have all its uniform clothing of the same patterns as laid down for the L.-Gds. Horse Regiment, but with white buttons. Horse furniture was left as before, unchanged [14].

14 March 1804 – Confirmation was given to a new table for the **Cavalier Guards Regiment**, which along with the order of 6 November 1803 presented above was the basis for all uniforms, accouterments, and weapons of this regiment being prescribed to be the same as for the L.-Gds. Horse Regiment except: white buttons; black collars and shoulder straps on the greatcoats; light colored [*svetlyi*] buttons on the riding trousers for all ranks; red shabracks and pistol carriers; galloon and all officer appointments silver; and black velvet for the collar, cuffs, and piping on the white turnbacks of officers' red undress coats, as well as for officers' undress shabracks and pistol carriers. Another difference from the L.-Gds. Horse Regiment was that silver embroidery in the form of buttonhole loops was left on the cuffs and skirttails of the red undress coats of Cavalier Guards officers (Illus. 2002) [15].

4 April 1804 – For everyday service, Cavalier Guards generals and field and company-grade officers were given dark-green **frock coats**, or undress coats, of the same pattern as described above for the Horse Guards, but with black velvet collar, cuffs, and piping (down the front coat opening, around the lining on the skirttails, and on the pocket flaps) with silver buttons (Illus. 2002) [16]. About this time, officers of both the Cavalier Guards and Horse Guards were ordered to wear hats with a buttonhole loop made from narrow galloon (the same color as the buttons) and with a tall plume (Illus. 2002) [17].

24 May 1804 – Shabracks and **pistol carriers** for lower ranks in the Cavalier Guards Regiment were ordered to have two rows of yellow woolen tape [*bason*] with a black cloth inlay between them (Illus. 2003). Lower ranks of the L.-Gds regiment were to have the same tape with a red cloth inlay (Illus. 2004). Officers of the Cavalier Guards Regiment were to have two rows of silver galloon with a black velvet inlay between them (Illus. 2005), and officers of the L.-Gds. Horse Regiment—two rows of gold galloon with a red cloth inlay (Illus. 2006) [18].

5 March 1805 – In the Cavalier Guards and L.-Gds. Horse Regiments **pistols** were ordered to be shorter than before and of the same pattern as pistols throughout the heavy Cavalry [19]. Also around this time, flankers [*flankera*] of the second of these regiments were given **rifles** [*shtutsera*] in place of carbines [*karabiny*] [20].

13 March 1806 – The same **rifles** were given to flankers in the Cavalier Guards Regiment [21].

10 October 1806 – In both regiments the previously authorized sheepskin **warm coats** [*fufaiki ili polushubki*] for lower ranks were withdrawn [22].

2 December 1806 – Lower ranks were ordered to cut off their queues and keep their **hair** short. Generals and field and company-grade officers, however, were in this matter allowed to proceed according to their personal inclination [23].

17 September 1807 — Generals and field and company-grade officers of both regiments were ordered to wear an **epaulette** [*epolet*] instead of a shoulder strap on the left shoulder of the *kolet* coat as well as of both undress coats. The epaulette was to be of the same pattern as established at this time for Guards infantry, of the same color as the buttons: silver in the Cavalier Guards and gold in the Horse Guards (Illus. 2007 and 2008). In this year Guards officers stopped carrying canes and wearing queues, and continued to powder their hair only for grand parades and appearances at HIGHEST Court [24].

26 January 1808 - Generals at parades, on designated calendar days [*tabelnye dni*], and at troop formations in general, in peacetime as well as during wartime, were ordered to wear the newly introduced **standard general's coat** [*obshchii gener-*

alskii mundir]. And with the regimental coat when not on duty, they were to have dark-green pants instead of white [25].
[Note by M.C.: The actual order referenced here (PSZ 22,784) actually reads differently:

> "The Sovereign Emperor orders that General Officers, when commanding just a single regiment of which they are the *Chef* (honorary colonel), and engaged in normal everyday guard mounts, may wear the regimental uniform, but at parades, on designated calendar days, and at all gatherings of several troop units, in peacetime as well as during wartime, they must wear the newly introduced standard General's coat, being allowed during the time they are not on duty to also wear dark-green cloth pants instead of white."

This order was to the entire army and did not mention any regiments in particular, and when properly interpreted I believe it spares us the ghastly image of dark-green pants being worn with white *kolet* coats.]

12 November 1808 – Cavalier Guards and Horse Guards field and company-grade officers, on normal everyday service when wearing the dark-green undress coat, were allowed to wear cloth **pants** of that same color [26].

26 November 1808 - Both regiments were ordered to have new-style flat **plumes** on their helmets while on campaign. For officers, noncommissioned officers, and privates, these were black, and for musicians—red. The previous chinstrap was replaced by new ones with flat brass **scales** (Illus. 2009 and 2010) [27]. In this same year, long-skirted dark-green *frock coats[sertuki]* were introduced for officers, with white lining, buttons the same color as on the *kolet* coat, and the same collar as on the dark-green undress coat, i.e. black velvet in the Cavalier Guards and dark-green cloth with red piping in the Horse Guards (Illus. 2010) [28].

6 December 1808 – Distinguished Officer Candidates [*estandart-yunkera*] and non-commissioned officers in both regiments were ordered to have two shoulder straps on their *kolet* coats instead of just one [29].

27 March 1809 – Instead of one **epaulette**, Cavalier Guards and Horse Guards generals and field and company-grade officers were ordered to have two, and with this the **aiguilettes** which they had worn were abolished (Illus. 2011) [30].

6 April 1809 – **Noncommissioned officers** were ordered to have **galloon** not on the lower and side edges of the collar, but on the upper and side edges (Illus. 2012) [31].

8 June 1809 - The plumage around the sides of **generals' hats** was discontinued and the former pattern of embroidered buttonhole was replaced with a new one made of four thick, twisted cords, of which the two middle ones were intertwined with each other in the form of a plait [32].

16 June 1810 - **Carbines** and **pistols** for both regiments were ordered to be made according to newly confirmed patterns. Both of these were of indentical caliber with infantry muskets (seven lines, measured in English inches [i.e. 0.7 inches - M.C.]), and along with this the first of these were prescribed to no longer be called carbines, but *cuirassier muskets [kirasirskiya ruzhya]* [33]. In this same year new-pattern **broadswords** [*palashi*] were introduced, with a brass hilt and all-iron scabbard, without any leather (Illus. 2012). Also, the high **plumes** on the generals' and officers' hats were shortened [34].

16 September 1811 – In both regiments, the rings on **cartridge pouches** for attaching them to the crossbelt were removed, and it was ordered that the pouches were to be worn in the fashion of infantry pouches, i.e. with the ends of the crossbelt put under the cartridge pouch [35].

23 September 1811 – A new pattern for **forage caps** was laid down, the same as introduced at this time for Army Cuirassier regiments: in the Cavalier Guards Regiment—white with a black band and piping, and in the L.-Gds. Horse Regiments—also white, with a red band and piping. Both ahd the squadron number in yellow cord on the band (Illus. 2013). Officers were prescribed the same forage cap but with a visor of black lacquered leather and without any number on the band [36].

In the **beginning of 1812** all ranks of the Cavalier Guards and Horse Guards regiments were ordered to make the **collars** on coats and greatcoats lower than before, and closed with small hooks (Illus. 2013). Private cuirassiers and non-commissioned officers were given black **cuirasses** with red lining, in all respects identical to those introduced at this time for Army Cuirassiers (Illus. 2014 and 2015). The thick **plumage** on officers' helmets for parades was completely abolished, and they were also ordered to have **gloves with gauntlets** (Illus. 2015) [37].

10 November 1812 - **Carbines** were withdrawn from both regiments, and subsequently the only firearms left were pistols and 16 rifles [*shtutsera*] in each squadron for the flankers [38].

27 December 1812 – The tassels and loops [*kisti i gaiki*] on the **sword knots** of the two new squadrons added to each regiment were ordered to be: 6th Squadron – red; 7th, reserve, Squadron – white with an admixture of red [39].

13 April 1813 – With the renaming of HIS MAJESTY's Leib-Cuirassier Regiment as the *Life-Guards Cuirassier Regiment* and its inclusion in the New, or Young, Guard, it kept all its previous uniform clothing, i.e. white with sky blue, with—for lower ranks—white buttonhole loops on the collars and cuffs, with a stripe of sky blue down the center (Illus. 2016 and 2018). Officer—who on this occasion were ordered to have pouch belts trimmed with silver galloon— had silver buttonhole loops, on the *kolet* coat (Illus. 2018) as well as on the white undress coat. The latter had, as before, a sky-blue collar, cuffs, and piping on the skirts and turnbacks. Along with this, shabracks and pistol carriers were ordered to be trimmed with blue [*svetlosinnii*] cloth with two rows of white lace for lower ranks (Illus. 2017) and two rows of silver galloon for officers [40].

7 December 1813 – Officers of the Cavalier Guards and L.-Gds. Cuirassier Regiments were ordered to have collars on the **frock coat** as follows: for the first—of dark-green cloth with red piping instead of being of black velvet, thus matching the L.-Gds. Horse Regiment, and for the

Soldiers of Russian Cuirassier Regiments 1812

second—dark-green with sky-blue piping, instead of being all sky blue. From this time, both in these two regiments as well as in the L.-Gds. Horse, **cuffsand cuff flaps** began to be trimmed with piping of the same color as the piping on the collar. Also, in the Cavalier Guards Regiment the black collar on the **greatcoat** was replaced by a gray cloth one with red cloth piping, with a black patch or tab [*nakladka ili klapan*] and—on the tab—a white button [41].

6 April 1814 – The double-breasted **undress coats**, red for officers of the Cavalier Guards and L.-Gds. Horse Regiment and white for the L.-Gds. Cuirassiers, were ordered to be single-breasted, with nine buttons. Likewise, the dark-green undress coats were to have nine buttons instead of eight (Illus. 2019) [42].

20 May 1814 – In the three regiments mentioned above, officers as well as lower ranks, were given single-breasted **dress coats** [*kolety*] with nine buttons, in place of the double-breasted ones. These had piping—in the same color as the collar—down the front and around the bottom to the tails, and white piping on the collar (Illus. 2020 and 2021). At this same time, the **campaign riding trousers** with buttons, used by officers since 1802, were replaced by new ones, grey as before, with two wide stripes [*lampasy*] and piping, of the same color as the dress coat's collar, and without leather on the inner seams (Illus. 2020) [43].

19 August 1814 - Similar **riding trousers**, except with leather on the seams, were also given to lower ranks (Illus. 2021) [44].

30 August 1814 – The L.-Gds. Cuirassier Regiment was ordered to have **helmets with stars** (Illus. 2022) and **bandoleers** [*pantalery*], of the same patterns as for the L.-Gds. Horse Regiment [45].

15 September 1814 - Each of these regiments was ordered to have 1120 **carbines** [*karabiny*] and 112 **rifles** [*shtutsera*]. In this same year a white band was added to the cockade on **officer's hats**, and which later was replaced with a silver one [46].

16 December 1815 – It was directed that **trumpeters** in these regiments have gray horses, and other ranks—dark colors [47]. In this same year the black velvet collars and piping on red **undress coats** in the Cavalier Guards Regiment were changed to dark-blue cloth. Cavalier Guards officers also had the **plumage** on their hats removed (Illus. 2023) [48].

29 December 1815 – Lower ranks of the Cavalier Guards, L.-Gds. Horse, and L.-Gds. Cuirassiers were ordered to have chamois [*zamshevyi*] **gloves** as previously, but with deerskin [*losinnyi*] guantlet cuffs [49].

24 January 1816 - **Scabbards** for officers' swords [*shpagi*] were ordered to be of black, lacquered leather [50].

13 Marcy 1816 – When assigning **remounts** to the Cavalier Guards, L.-Gds. Horse, and L.-Gds. Cuirassiers, it was ordered that chestnuts, blacks, bays, browns, sorrels, and grays [*gnedye, voronye, karie, burye, ryzhie i serye*] be selected. The last color was only for trumpeters. Care was to be taken that the horses were not less than 2 arshins 2-1/2 vershoks [64-3/4 inches] high [51].

21 September 1816 - For carrying rifles when in formation, carabiniers were ordered to have **bandoleers** with hooks on which to hang the rifles, as used at this time in Horse-Jäger and Lancer regiments and related above for Army Cuirassiers [52].

6 May 1817 – **Trumpeters** in the Cavalier Guards and L.-Gds. Horse were ordered to trim their dress coats with yellow tape [*bason*] with a red stripe or light, and in the L.-Gds. Cuirassiers—with white tape with a sky-blue stripe or light. Their swallows' nests or wings were to be according to the color of the collar: red in the first two regiments and sky blue in the last (Illus. 2024) [53].

8 August 1817 - The **scales on chinstraps** were ordered to be raised or convex, instead of flat [54].

2 March 1818 – The newly established *L.-Gds. Podolia Cuirassier Regiment* in Warsaw was prescribed to have: white *kolet* coat of the normal cuirassier pattern, with yellow cloth collar, cuffs, shoulder straps, piping, and lining on the tails and turnbacks, and white buttons. On both sides of the collar was a single tab of dark-blue cloth with a buttonhole loop (of yellow guards tape for lower ranks and in silver for officers) and button. Deerskin pants; gray riding trousers with yellow stripes and piping; yellow shabrack and pistol carriers, these being of cloth, with guards-pattern stars and trimmed around with dark-blue cloth and two rows of yellow tape, or silver galloon for officers. All other items of uniform clothing were as used in the Cavalier Guards, L.-Gds. Horse, and L.-Gds. Cuirassiers, except that the galloon on officers' pouches was silver with yellow piping (Illus. 2025, 2026, 2027, and 2028). Horses in this regiment were blacks [55].

8 November 1818 – To bring them into conformity with other Guards regiments, **non-commissioned officers** of the Cavalier Guards, L.-Gds. Horse, and L.-Gds. Cuirassiers were ordered to have only one buttonhole loop on their collar instead of two (Illus. 2029) [56].

Soldiers of Russian Cuirassier Regiments 1812

In this same year the supporting **straps on cuirasses** were ordered to be longer than before, as was first introduced in the Podolia Regiment (Illus. 2025, 2026, and 2027) [57].

In 1820 – For **trumpeters** in all four regiments, the chevrons on their coats began to be sewn on closer together than previously, and tape was put all around the collar. For all ranks, white piping was removed from *kolet* **coat collars** (Illus. 2030) [58].

25 July 1822 – In the Cavalier Guards Regiment the black trim on red **shabracks** and **pistol carriers** was ordered to be changed to dark-blue cloth. The tab or patch on **greatcoat collars** was changed from black to red cloth, and **forage caps** were to have a red band and black piping (Illus. 2031) [59].

In March of 1823 – With the decision that Guards Cavalry regiments have **horses** of one color, the Cavalier Guards Regiment was ordered to have chestnuts, the L.-Gds. Horse and L.-Gds. Podolia Cuirassiers—blacks, and the L.-Gds. Cuirassiers—sorrels [60].

29 March 1825 - For combatant lower ranks, for faultless service, there were established **stripes** [*nashivki*] to be sewn on the left sleeve: for 10 years service—one, for 15 years—two, for 20 years—three; one over the other, all of yellow tape [*tesma*] [61].

XXXIV. GUARDS DRAGOONS.
[Gvardeiskie draguny.]

12 January 1809 – The newly formed **L.-Gds. Dragoon Regiment** was ordered to have the exact same uniform as received by the L.-Gds. Lithuania Regiment in 1811, except that the cuffs were slit, without flaps, and had two buttonhole loops and buttons. Helmets were the same pattern as for the Cavalier Guards and Horse Guards. Badges on the pouches were the same as for Guards heavey infantry. Saddlecloths [*valtrapy*] were dark green, with lower ranks having red cloth trim, monograms, and crowns, and two rows of yellow woolen on the trim. Officers had red cloth trim with two rows of gold galloon and silver stars. All else in regard to uniforms, accouterments, and weapons was prescribed to be the same as used in Army Dragoon regiments (Illus. 2032, 2033, and 2034). For everyday dress [*v-budni*] officers wore: dark-green pants instead of white; hats with a tall white plume; cavalry swords [*shpagi*] with a silver sword knot (Illus. 2035), and frock coats. This last item was of the same pattern as for the L.-Gds. Preobrazhenskii and Lithuania Regiments [62].

16 June 1810 – Musketoons [*mushkety*] and pistols for the regiment were ordered to be made according to the newly confirmed pattern. Both of them were of the same caliber as infantry muskets (seven lines, measured in English inches), and along with this the first weapon was prescribed not to be called a musketoon, but a **dragoon musket** [*dragunskoe ruzh'e*] [63]. Also in this year, the **plumes** on the hats of generals and officers were shortened [64].

16 September 1811 – For combatant lower ranks, all buckles, prongs, and end pieces on cartridge-pouch belts, the hooks for muskets, and the rings for pouches—were all removed, and it was ordered that the **pouches** be worn in the manner of infantry cartridge pouches, i.e. passing the end of the crossbelt under the pouch [65].

23 September 1811 – A new pattern of **forage cap** was confirmed for the L.-Gds. Dragoon Regiment, identical with that established at this time for the other Guards regiments. It was dark green in color with a red band and a yellow squadron number on the band. Officers wore the same caps but without a number, with a visor of black lacquered leather [66].

5 December 1811 – **Kettledrums** were abolished in the L.-Gds. Dragoon Regiment [67].

In the beginning of 1812, collars on tailcoats, greatcoats, and officers' frock coats were ordered to be lower than currently, fastened by little hooks, with the same sewn-on lace as the L.-Gds. Lithuania Regiment had at this time, i.e. in yellow with red stripes for lower ranks, and gold, as previously, for officers (Illus. 2036 and 2037). In addition, the thick **plumage** on officers' helmets for parades was abolished [68].

10 November 1812 – **Muskets** were withdrawn, and consequently the Leib-Dragoons' firearms consisted only of pistols, except for flankers (16 in each squadron), who also had rifles [69].

27 December 1812 – The squadrons newly added to the L.-Gds. Dragoon Regiment were ordered to have **sword knot** tassels and slides as follows: 6th Squadron – red, 7th, reserve – white with an admixture of red [70].

20 May 1814 – Officers' **riding trousers** [*reituzy*] with buttons, as used since the regiment was formed, were replaced by new ones of the previous gray color, with wide red stripes and piping and without leather along the inside seams [71].

19 August 1814 – Similar **riding trousers**, except with leather reinforcements, were given to lower ranks [72].

14 September 1814 – In addition to the 112 rifles from 1812, the regiment was given 1120 **muskets** [*ruzh'ya*]. In this same year a white band was added to the **cockade** on officer's hats, and which was later replaced with by silver one [72].

16 December 1815 - **Trumpeters** were oredered to have grey horses, and other ranks — dark colors [74].

13 March 1816 - When assigning **remounts** to the L.-Gds. Dragoon Regiment, it was ordered that chestnuts, blacks, bays, browns, sorrels, and grays be selected. The last color was only for trumpeters. Care was to be taken that the horses were not less than 2 arshins 1 vershok [57-3/4 inches] high, and no more than 2 arshins 3 vershoks [61-1/4 inches] [75].

28 February 1817 – When in formation or in full uniform [*polnaya forma*], officers were ordered to have **pouches** [*lyadunki*] of the pattern used by Army Dragoon and Horse-Jäger regiments, with gold galloon on the belt and a silver badge, buckle, prong, end piece, prickers, and chain [76].

8 March 1817 – The regiment was given **new uniforms** of the pattern used at this time in Army Dragoon regiments, but keeping the previous colors of the lapels, the buttonhole loops, and guards badge on the shako (Illus. 2038 and 2039) [77].

14 March 1817 - **Field and company-grade officers** of the L.-Gds. Dragoon Reg., when in formation with troops or when wearing sashes, were ordered to be in dress coats with short tails without pocket flaps, and wearing cartridge pouches [78].

6 May 1817 – **Trumpeters** were ordered to have tape sewn onto their coats, yellow with thin red stripes, and wings or shoulder pieces [*kryl'tsa ili naplechniki*] of the same color as the collar—red (Illus. 2040) [79].

16 February 1819 – For use on campaign, the regiment was given **covers** for shakos and plumes, identical to those established at this same time for Army Dragoon regiments [80].

28 February 1819 – Generals and field and company-grade officers were given a new pattern of **saber**, with a brass hilt instead of iron, with a black leather grip wound round with brass wire, and with an iron scabbard. Officers possessing a gold saber awarded for military distinction were ordered to have a gold grip in the hilt; bands on the scabbard and the rings on these bands were to be brass, and on the arcs of the guard was inscribed "for courage" ["*za khrabrost*"] (Illus. 2041) [81].

20 February 1820 – Instead of hair plumes on the shakos, the regiment was directed to have small oblong plumes or **pompons** [*sultanchiki ili pompony*]: for lower ranks—yellow, of wool; for officers—silver. However, these were not to be worn until specifically ordered, and meanwhile only the previous pompon [*repeiki*] was to be on the shako, without a plume (Illus. 2041) [82].

7 August 1820 – Generals and field and company-grade officers of the L.-Gds. Dragoon Regiment were allowed to wear **moustaches** [83]. Also, beginning in this year the tape on **musicians' coats** began to be worn more closely together and around the whole collar (Illus. 2041) [84].

In March of 1823 - With the introduction of the rule that Guards Cavalry regiments have **horses** of one color, the L.-Gds. Dragoon Regiment was ordered to have blacks [85].

18 December 1823 – In was ordered that the **pompons** prescribed in 1820 be worn (Illus. 2042) [86].

29 March 1825 –For faultless service, **chevrons** sewn on the left sleeve were established for combatant lower ranks: for 10 years of service—one; for 15 years—two; and for 20—three, one over the other; all of yellow tape [87].

18 August 1825 – The oblong **pompons** of lower ranks and officers were changed to round ones (Illus. 2043) [88].

Soldiers and officer of Russian Guard cavalry Regiments - Above a Russian Dragoon

XXXV. GUARDS HORSE-JÄGERS.
[Gvardeiskie konnye yegerya.]

26 June 1814 – The newly formed *Life-Guards Horse-Jäger Regiment* was ordered to have the same uniforms, accouterments, and arms as issued at this time to Army Horse Jägers, but with a red collar, cuffs, shoulder straps, piping, and trim on the skirttails and pants. Four buttonhole loops were prescribed for the collar, and one on each cuff; for lower ranks—whitewith a red light; for officers—silver. The shako had a guards pattern badge, and its cords were white and its pompon green. The pouch badge was the guards pattern with an eight-pointed star. The saddlecloth was red, having for lower ranks two rows of white tape on a dark-green backing, with red monograms and crowns trimmed with thin white cord (Illus. 2044 and 2045), and for officers two rows of silver galloon on the same dark-green backing, and with silver stars (Illus. 2046). When in formation on parade officers wore coats with short tails, but for everyday wear and when not in formation with long tails [89].

19 August 1814 – Lower ranks, instead of the prescribed gray riding trousers for campaign use, with covered buttons on the side seams, were ordered to have **trousers** with wide red stripes and piping, and leather along the inner seams. Officers had the same riding trousers that they used since the founding of the regiment, except without leather [90].

In the same year of 1814 – Cockades on officers' hats were ordered to have a white ribbon around them, later changed to silver [91].

1 February 1816 – In place of red **collars**, all lower ranks were given dark-green ones with red piping and likewise red tabs. The collars on dress coats were to have one buttonhole loop on each side—white for lower ranks and silver for officers, with a button (Illus. 2047). Also, the colors of the **saddlecloth** were prescribed to be reversed from previously: instead of red with dark green, they were to be dark green with red trim, with the monograms for lower ranks remaining as before, without change (Illus. 2047) [92].

13 March 1816 – When assigning **remounts** to the L.-Gds. Horse-Jäger Regiment, it was ordered that any color horse be selected except light bays [*solovye*], Isabellas [*izabely*, i.e. palominos], spotted [*chubarye*], sorrel or light-brown Tatar breeds [*kaurye*], light chestnuts tending to yellow [*savrasye*], and pigeon grays or ash colors [*golubye*] [93].

17 March 1817 – On officers' **undress tailcoats** [*vitse-mundiry*], i.e. the dress coats with long tails [*mundiry s dlinnymi faldami*], the turnbacks on the tails were ordered to be dark green, while the piping on the turnbacks and on the elongated pocket flaps was to be red (Illus. 2048) [94]. Also, officers were given frock coats [*sertuki*] with the same collar as on the dress coat but without buttonhole loops, and with dark-green lining (Illus. 2049).

6 May 1817 – **Trumpeters** were ordered to have red wings or shoulder pieces instead of dark green, while the sewn-on tape was white, as before, but with a thin red stripe down the middle (Illus. 2050) [95]. In this same year all combatant lower ranks were given a **shako** higher than previously, with a flat top and convex chinscales. Privates' **carbines** without bayonets were replaced with new weapons, with bayonets, that received the name *Horse-Jäger muskets* [*Konno-Yegerskiya ruzh'ya*]. These were identical to those introduced at this time for Army Horse Jägers (Illus. 2050) [96].

16 February 1819 – When on campaign or in camp, the L.-Gds. Horse-Jäger Regiment was ordered to have **covers** on shakos and plumes, identical to those established at this time for Army Dragoon and Horse-Jäger regiments [97].

28 February 1819 – Generals and field and company-grade officers were given new **sabers** of the same pattern as that established at this time for the L.-Gds. Dragoon Regiment [98].

4 April 1819 – In the L.-Gds. Horse-Jäger Regiment the dark-green pants were ordered to have sewn-on cuffs of black leather, as for Dragoons [99].

20 February 1820 – It was directed that the shakos in the L.-Gds. Horse-Jäger Regiment, instead of hair plumes, have small oblong plumes or **pompons** [*sultanchiki ili pomony*]: of white wool for lower ranks, and silver for officers. However, these were not to be worn until so ordered, and until then the shakos were left with just the old pompons [*repeiki*] without plumes [100]. From this same year the tape on trumpeters' coats began to be sewn on closer together, and around the entire collar (Illus. 2051) [101].

In March 1823 – With the introduction of the rule that Guards Cavalry regiments have **horses** of one color, the L.-Gds. Horse-Jäger Regiment was ordered to have grays [102].

18 December 1823 – It was ordered to wear the **pompons** proposed in 1820 (Illus. 2052) [103].

29 March 1825 - For faultless service, **chevrons** sewn on the left sleeve were established for combatant lower ranks: for 10 years of service — one; for 15 years — two; and for 20 — three, one over the other; all of yellow tape [104].

18 August 1825 – For both lower ranks and officers the oblong **pompons** were changed to round (Illus. 2053) [105].

The Zar Alexander Ist and his Cossack in Paris 1814

NOTES

(1) *Complete Collection of Laws* [*Polnoe Sobranie Zakonov*, henceforth PSZ], Vol. XXVI, pg. 609, No 19,826.

(2) From the files of the War Ministry's Commissariat Department.

(3) PSZ Vol. XLIV, pt. II, regulation for uniforms, pg. 72, No 19,950.

(4) The Archive of the the War Ministry's Inspection Department, in the book of orders issued by the Government Military Collegium in 1801.

(5) PSZ Vol. XLIV, Pt. II, sect. 4, regulations for uniforms, pg. 45, No 20,164.

(6) Drawings held in the SOVEREIGN EMPEROR's Own Library, catalogued as No 246, and statements by contemporaries.

(7) Ditto.

(8) Ditto.

(9) Highest confirmed table of uniforms, accouterments, and weapons for the Life-Guards Horse Regiment, 29 December 1802; drawings located in the SOVEREIGN EMPEROR'S Own Library, catalogued under No 246; various uniforms and other items preserved up to the present time, and statements by contemporaries.

(10) These drum banners are now preserved in HIS IMPERIAL MAJESTY'S Own Arsenal, in the Anichkov Palace.

(11) Undress coats and shabracks with pistol carriers, preserved up to the present time, and statements by contemporaries.

(12) From the files of the War Ministry's Commissariat Department.

(13) PSZ Vol. XXVII, pg. 934, No 20,989, and actual helmets preserved up to the present time.

(14) Announcement by the Government Military Collegium to the Military Commission, 6 November 1803.

(15) Highest confirmed table of uniforms, accouterments, and weapons for Cavalier Guards Regiment, 14 March 1804, and statements by contemporaries.

(16) Determination made by the Government Military Collegium, 4 April 1804, and statements by contemporaries.

(17) Statements by contemporaries.

(18) From the files of the War Ministry's Commissariat Department, and shabracks with pistol carriers preserved up to the present time.

(19) PSZ Vol. XXVII, pg. 887, No 21,651.

(20) Statements by contemporaries.

(21) Report by the St.-Petersburg Commissariat Commission to the Government Military Collegium, 13 March 1806.

(22) From the files of the War Ministry's Commissariat Department.

(23) PSZ Vol. XXIX, pg. 21, No 22,382.

(24) From the files of the War Ministry's Commissariat Department; uniforms from that time, preserved up to now, and statements by contemporaries.

(25) PSZ Vol. XXX, pg. 45, No 22,784.

(26) From the files of the War Ministry's Commissariat Department.

(27) PSZ Vol. XLIV, pg. 13, No 23,373; actual helmets preserved in Arsenals; drawings from that time, and statements by contemporaries.

(28) Statements by contemporaries.

(29) PSZ Vol. XLIV, pg. 13, No 23,386.

(30) Ibid., Vol. XLIV, pg. 13, No 23,548.

(31) From the files of the War Ministry's Commissariat Department.

(32) PSZ Vol. XXX, pg. 1006, No. 23,695.

(33) Ibid., Vol. XXXI, pg. 215, No 24,263.

(34) Statements by contemporaries.

(35) PSZ Vol. XLIV, pg. 54, No 24,774.

(36) PSZ Vol. XLIV, pg. 69, No 24,769, and statements by contemporaries.

(37) Statements by contemporaries; contemporary portraits and drawings, and actual items preserved in various Arsenals or in the possession of private persons.

(38) PSZ Vol. XXXII, pg. 454, No 25,262, and statements by contemporaries.

(39) From the files of the War Ministry's Commissariat Department.

(40) See above, in Vol. XI, under the description of uniforms for Army Cuirassier regiments, through 3 April 1813.

(41) PSZ Vol. XLIV, pg. 100, Nos 25,489 and 25,490, and statements by contemporaries.

(42) PSZ Vol. XLIV, pg. 133, No 25,565.

(43) PSZ Vol. XLIV, pg. 133, No 25,589, and statements by contemporaries.

(44) Ibid., Vol. XXXII, pg. 876, No 25,644, and statements by contemporaries.

(45) PSZ Vol. XXXII, pg. 906, No 25,670.

(46) From the files of the War Ministry's Commissariat Department, and statements by contemporaries.

(47) Ditto.

(48) Ditto.

(49) PSZ Vol. XLIV, pg. 134, No 27,770, and model pattern gloves preserved at the War Ministry's Commissariat Department.

(50) Ibid., Vol. XXXIII, pg. 1029, No 26,441.

(51) Ibid., pg. 543, No 26,192.

(52) HIGHEST Order and statements by contemporaries.

(53) From the files of the War Ministry's Commissariat Department.

(54) Ditto.

(55) PSZ Vol. XLIV, pg. 103, No 27,298, and from the files of the War Ministry's Commissariat Department.

(56) From the files of the War Ministry's Commissariat Department.

(57) Statements by contemporaries, and cuirasses preserved up to the present time in various Arsenals.

(58) From the files of the War Ministry's Commissariat Department, and actual uniform coats preserved up to the present time.

(59) PSZ Vol. XLIV, pg. 100, No 29,140, and from the files of the War Ministry's Commissariat Department.

(60) From the files of the War Ministry's Commissariat Department.

(61) PSZ Vol. XL, pg. 188, No 30,309.

(62) HighestConfirmed table of uniforms, accouterments, and weapons for the L.-Gds. Dragoon Regiment, 12 December 1809; uniforms of that time, preserved up to the present time, and statements by contemporaries.

(63) PSZ Vol. XXXI, pg. 215, No 24,263.

(64) Statements by contemporaries.

(65) PSZ Vol. XLIV, pg. 54, No 24,774, and from the files of the War Ministry's Commissariat Department.

(66) From the files of the same Department.

(67) PSZ Vol. XLIV, pg. 910, No 24,899.

(68) Statements by contemporaries, and from the files of the War Ministry's Commissariat Department.

(69) PSZ Vol. XXXII, pg. 454, No 25,262.

(70) Ibid., Vol. XLIV, pg. 50 No 25,278.

(71) From the files of the War Ministry's Commissariat Department.

(72) Ditto.

(73) Ditto.

(74) From the files of the same Department.

(75) PSZ Vol. XXIII, pg. 549, No 26,192.

(76) PSZ Vol. XLIV, pg. 101, No 26,727, and actual pouches preserved from that time.

(77) Ibid., pg. 101, No 26,723, and model pattern uniforms preserved at the War Ministry's Commissariat Department.

(78) PSZ Vol. XLIV, pg. 101, No 26,727.

(79) From the files of the War Ministry's Commissariat Department.

(80) PSZ Vol. XLIV, pg. 101, No 27,681.

(81) Order from the Chief of HIS IMPERIAL MAJESTY's Main Staff, 28 February 1819, No 15, and actual sabers.

(82) From the files of the War Ministry's Commissariat Department.

(83) PSZ Vol. XXXVII, pg. 409, No 28,374.

(84) From the Archive files of the War Ministry's Commissariat Department.

(85) Ditto.

(86) Ditto.

(87) PSZ Vol. XL, pg. 188, No 30,309.

(88) From the files of the War Ministry's Commissariat Department.

(89) PSZ Vol. XLIV, pg. 101, No 26,611; model pattern uniforms preserved at the War Ministry's Commissariat Department, and statements by contemporaries.

(90) From the files of the War Ministry's Commissariat Department.

(91) Ditto, and statements by contemporaries.

(92) From the files of the War Ministry's Commissariat Department.

(93) PSZ Vol. XXXIII, pg. 543, No 26,192.

(94) From the files of the War Ministry's Commissariat Department.

(95) Ditto.

(96) Ditto, and actual horse-jäger muskets from that time.

(97) PSZ Vol. XLIV, pg. 101, No 27,681.

(98) Order from the Chief of HIS IMPERIAL MAJESTY's Main Staff, 28 February 1819, No 15, and actual sabers.

(99) From the files of the War Ministry's Commissariat Department.

(100) Ditto.

(101) Ditto.

(102) Ditto.

(103) Ditto.

(104) PSZ Vol. XL, pg. 188, No 30,309.

(105) From the files of the War Ministry's Commissariat Department.

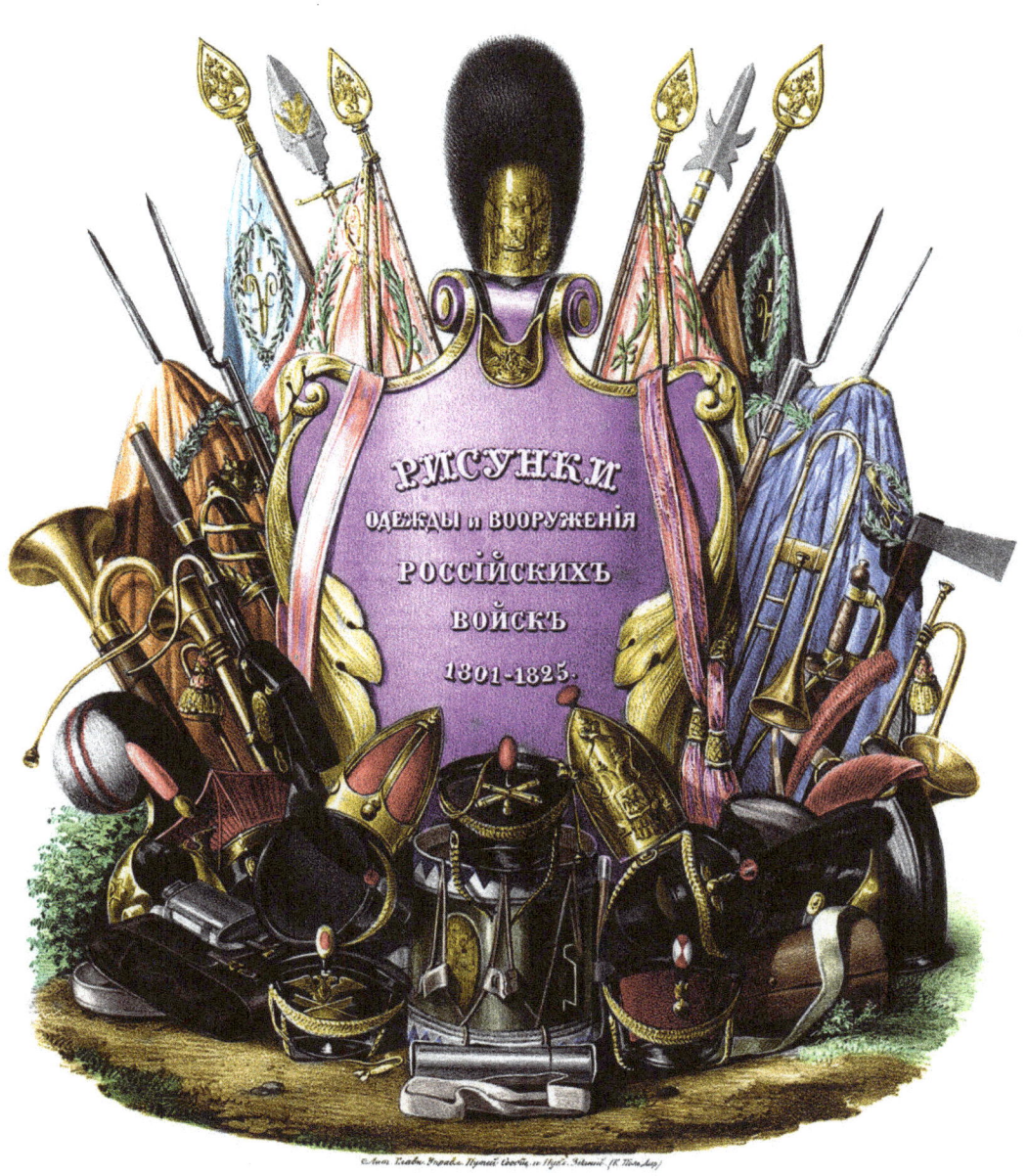

РИСУНКИ
ОДЕЖДЫ и ВООРУЖЕНІЯ
РОССІЙСКИХЪ
ВОЙСКЪ
1301-1825.

PLATES LIST OF ILLUSTRATIONS

2021. Non-Commissioned Officers., L.-Gds. Horse Regiment, and L.-Gds. Cuirassier Reg., 1814-1820.

2022. Field-Grade Officer and Private. L.-Gds. Cuirassier Regiment, 1814-1820.

2023. General. Cavalier Guards Regiment, 1815-1825.

2024. Trumpeters. Cavalier Guards Regiment, L.-Gds. Horse Regiment, and L.-Gds. Cuirassier Regiment, 1817-1820

2025. Private. L.-Gds. Podolia Cuirassier Regiment, 1818-1820. *Note. The yellow tape along the dark-blue insert on shabracks and pistol carriers was later replaced by white.*

2026. Non-Commissioned Officer. L.-Gds. Podolia Cuirassier Regiment, 1818-1820.

2027. Field-Grade Officer. L.-Gds. Podolia Cuirassier Regiment, 1818-1820.

2028. Embroidery on officers' coats in the L.-Gds. Podolia Cuirassier Regiment, since 1818.

2029. Non-Commissioned Officer. Cavalier Guards Regiment, 1818-1820.

2030. Trumpeters. L.-Gds. Cuirassier Regiment and L.-Gds. Podolia Cuirassier Regiment, 1820-1825.

2031. Cavalier Guardsman, 1822-1825.

2032. Private. L.-Gds. Dragoon Regiment, 1809-1811.

2033. Non-Commissioned Officer and Staff-Trumpeter. L.-Gds. Dragoon Regiment, 1809-1811.

2034. Company-Grade Officer. L.-Gds. Dragoon Regiment, 1809-1811.

2035. Field-Grade Officer. L.-Gds. Dragoon Regiment, 1809-1811.

2036. Private. L.-Gds. Dragoon Regiment, 1812-1817.

2037. Company-Grade Officer. L.-Gds. Dragoon Regiment, 1812-1817.

2038. Non-Commissioned Officer and Company-Grade Officer. L.-Gds. Dragoon Reg., 1817-1819.

2039. Private. L.-Gds. Dragoon Regiment, 1817-1819.

2040. Trumpeter. L.-Gds. Dragoon Regiment, 1817-1820.

2041-42. Staff-Trumpeter and Trumpeter. L.-Gds. Dragoon Regiment, 1823-1825.

2043. Private and Company-Grade Officer. L.-Gds. Dragoon Regiment, 1825.

2044. Private. L.-Gds. Horse-Jäger Regiment, 1814-1816.

2045. Non-Commissioned Officer. L.-Gds. Horse-Jäger Regiment, 1814-1816.

2046. Company-Grade Officer. L.-Gds. Horse-Jäger Regiment, 1814-1816.

2047a. Embroidery on officers' coats in the L.-Gds. Horse-Jäger Regiment, since 1816.

2047b. Field-Grade Officer and Company-Grade Officers. L.-Gds. Horse-Jäger Regiment, 1816-1819.

2048. Company-Grade Officer. L.-Gds. Horse-Jäger Regiment, 1817-1819.

2049. Company-Grade Officer. L.-Gds. Horse-Jäger Regiment, 1817-1819.

2050. Trumpeter and Private. L.-Gds. Horse-Jäger Regiment, 1817-1819.

2051. Trumpeter. L.-Gds. Horse-Jäger Regiment, 1820-1825.

2052. Field-Grade Officer and Private. L.-Gds. Horse-Jäger Regiment, 1823-1825.

2053. Non-Commissioned Officer and Company-Grade Officer. L.-Gds. Horse-Jäger Regiment, 1825.

Privates. Cavalier Guards Regiment, 1801-1803

Non-Commissioned Officer. Cavalier Guards Regiment, 1802-1803

1989

Company-Grade Officer. Cavalier Guards Regiment, 1802-1803

27

Officer's cartridge pouch, Cavalier Guards Regiment, 1801-1803 -Kettledrum banner, L.-Gds. Horse Regimenta, 1802-1825 - Stars for helmets in the Guards Cavalry, since 1803. a. Lower ranks. b. Officers Stars for helmets in the Guards Cavalry, since 1803. a. Lower ranks. b. Office Stars for helmets in the Guards Cavalry, since 1803. a. Lower ranks. b. Officers

1991

Private. L.-Gds. Horse Regiment, 1802-1803

29

Trumpeter and Staff-Trumpeter. L.-Gds. Horse Regiment, 1802-1803

1993

Company-Grade Officer. L.-Gds. Horse Regiment, 1802-1803

1994

General. L.-Gds. Horse Regiment, 1802-1803

Company-Grade Officers. L.-Gds. Horse Regiment, 1802-1804

1997

Company-Grade Officer. L.-Gds. Horse Regiment, 1802-1807

1998

Private. Cavalier Guards Regiment, 1803

Staff-Trumpeter and Non-Commissioned Officer. L.-Gds. Horse Regiment, 1803-1806

General. Cavalier Guards Regiment, 1803-1806

Company-Grade Officers. Cavalier Guards Regiment, 1804-1806

2003

Private. Cavalier Guards Regiment, 1804-1806

Non-Commissioned Officer. L.-Gds. Horse Regiment, 1804-1806

2005

Company-Grade Officer. Cavalier Guards Regiment, 1804-1807

41

General. L.-Gds Horse Regiment, 1804-1806

2007

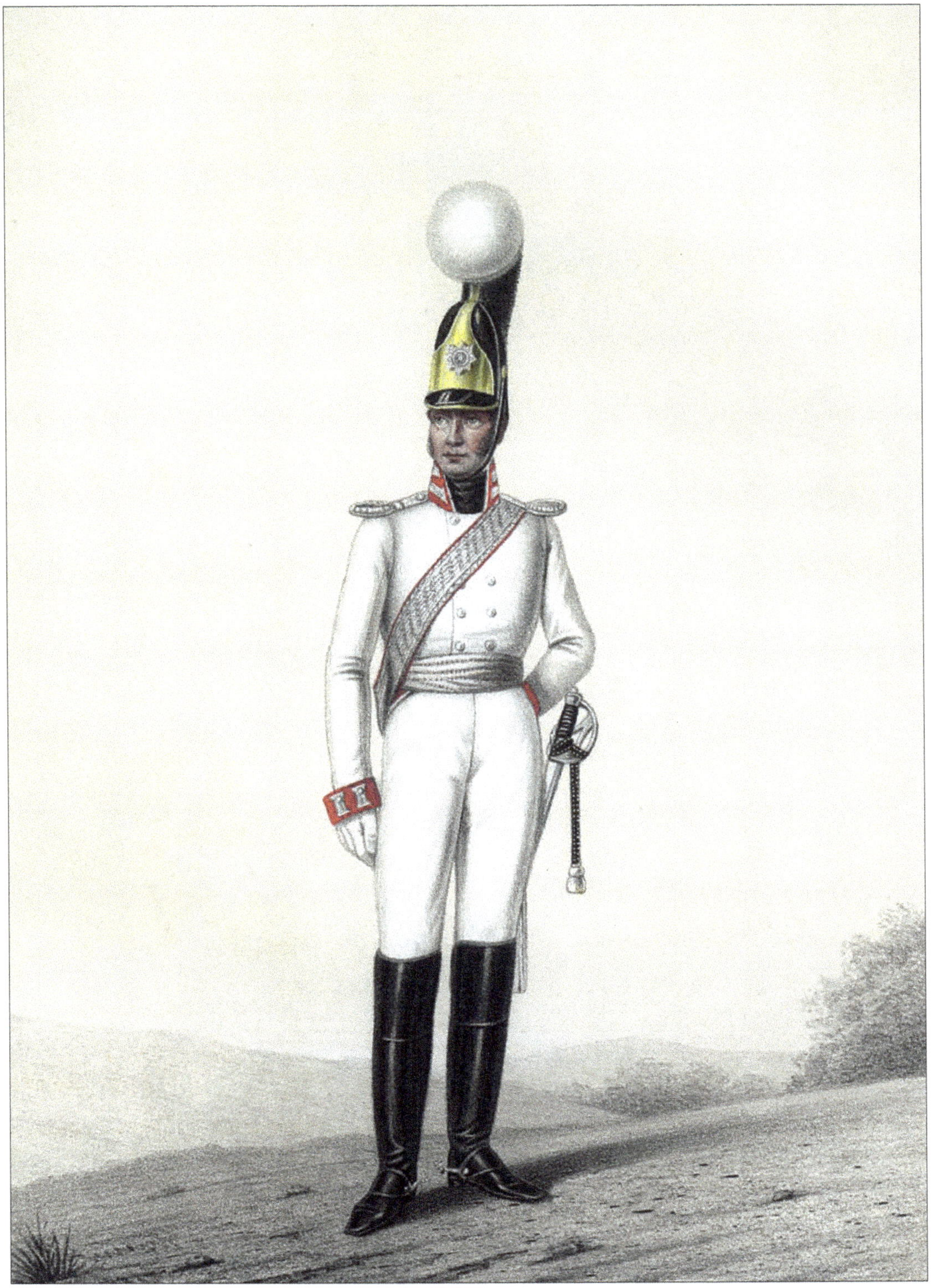

Company-Grade Officer. Cavalier Guards Regiment, 1807-1809

2008

Company-Grade Officer. L.-Gds Horse Regiment, 1807-18

2009

Private of the Cavalier Guards Regiment and Trumpeter of the L.-Gds Horse Regiment, 1808-180

Field-Grade Officers. Cavalier Guards Regiment and L.-Gds Horse Regiment, 1808-1809

Field-Grade Officers. Cavalier Guards Regiment and L.-Gds Horse Regiment, 1809-1811

Non-Commissioned Officer. L.-Gds Horse Regiment, 1809-1811

Non-Commissioned Officer. L.-Gds Horse Regiment, 1812-1814

Private. Cavalier Guards Regiment, 1812-1820

Field-Grade Officer. L.-Gds. Horse Regiment, 1812-1820

2016

Private. L.-Gds. Cuirassier Regiment, 1813-1814. Note. The white insert between the rows of tape on shabracks and pistol carriers was later replaced by blue

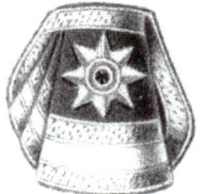 

Officers shabracks and pistol carriers of the L.-Gds. Cuirassiers since 1813. Note. The white insert between the galloon was later replaced by blue

Field-Grade Officer and Trumpeter. L.-Gd. Cuirassier Regiment, 1813-1814

Company-Grade Officers. Cavalier Guards Regiment, L.-Gds. Horse Regiment, and L.-Gds. Cuirassier Regiment, 1814-1825

Company-Grade Officers. Cavalier Guards Regiment, L.-Gds. Horse Regiment, and L.-Gds. Cuirassier Regiment, 1814-1820Gds. Moscow Regiment), since 1812

Non-Commissioned Officers., L.-Gds. Horse Regiment, and L.-Gds. Cuirassier Regiment, 1814-1820

Field-Grade Officer and Private. L.-Gds. Cuirassier Regiment, 1814-1820

General. Cavalier Guards Regiment, 1815-1825

Trumpeters. Cavalier Guards Regiment, L.-Gds. Horse Regiment, and L.-Gds. Cuirassier Regiment, 1817-1820

Private. L.-Gds. Podolia Cuirassier Regiment, 1818-1820. Note. The yellow tape along the dark-blue insert on shabracks and pistol carriers was later replaced by white

2026

Non-Commissioned Officer. L.-Gds. Podolia Cuirassier Regiment, 1818-1820

Field-Grade Officer. L.-Gds. Podolia Cuirassier Regiment, 1818-1820

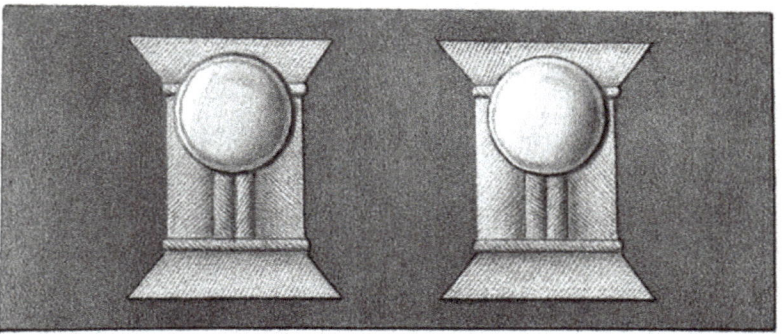

Embroidery on officers' coats in the L.-Gds. Podolia Cuirassier Regiment, since 1818

2029

Non-Commissioned Officer. Cavalier Guards Regiment, 1818-1820

Trumpeters. L.-Gds. Cuirassier Regiment and L.-Gds. Podolia Cuirassier Regiment, 1820-1825

2031

Cavalier Guardsman, 1822-1825

2032

Private. L.-Gds. Dragoon Regiment, 1809-1811.

Non-Commissioned Officer and Staff-Trumpeter. L.-Gds. Dragoon Regiment, 1809-1811

Company-Grade Officer. L.-Gds. Dragoon Regiment, 1809-1811

2035

Field-Grade Officer. L.-Gds. Dragoon Regiment, 1809-1811

2036

Private. L.-Gds. Dragoon Regiment, 1812-1817

2037

Company-Grade Officer. L.-Gds. Dragoon Regiment, 1812-1817

73

2038

Non-Commissioned Officer and Company-Grade Officer. L.-Gds. Dragoon Regiment, 1817-1819

74

2039

Private. L.-Gds. Dragoon Regiment, 1817-1819

75

Trumpeter. L.-Gds. Dragoon Regiment, 1817-1820

Staff-Trumpeter and Trumpeter. L.-Gds. Dragoon Regiment, 1823-18

2043

Private and Company-Grade Officer. L.-Gds. Dragoon Regiment, 1825

2044

Private. L.-Gds. Horse-Jäger Regiment, 1814-1816

2045

Non-Commissioned Officer. L.-Gds. Horse-Jäger Regiment, 1814-1816

2046

Company-Grade Officer. L.-Gds. Horse-Jäger Regiment, 1814-1816.

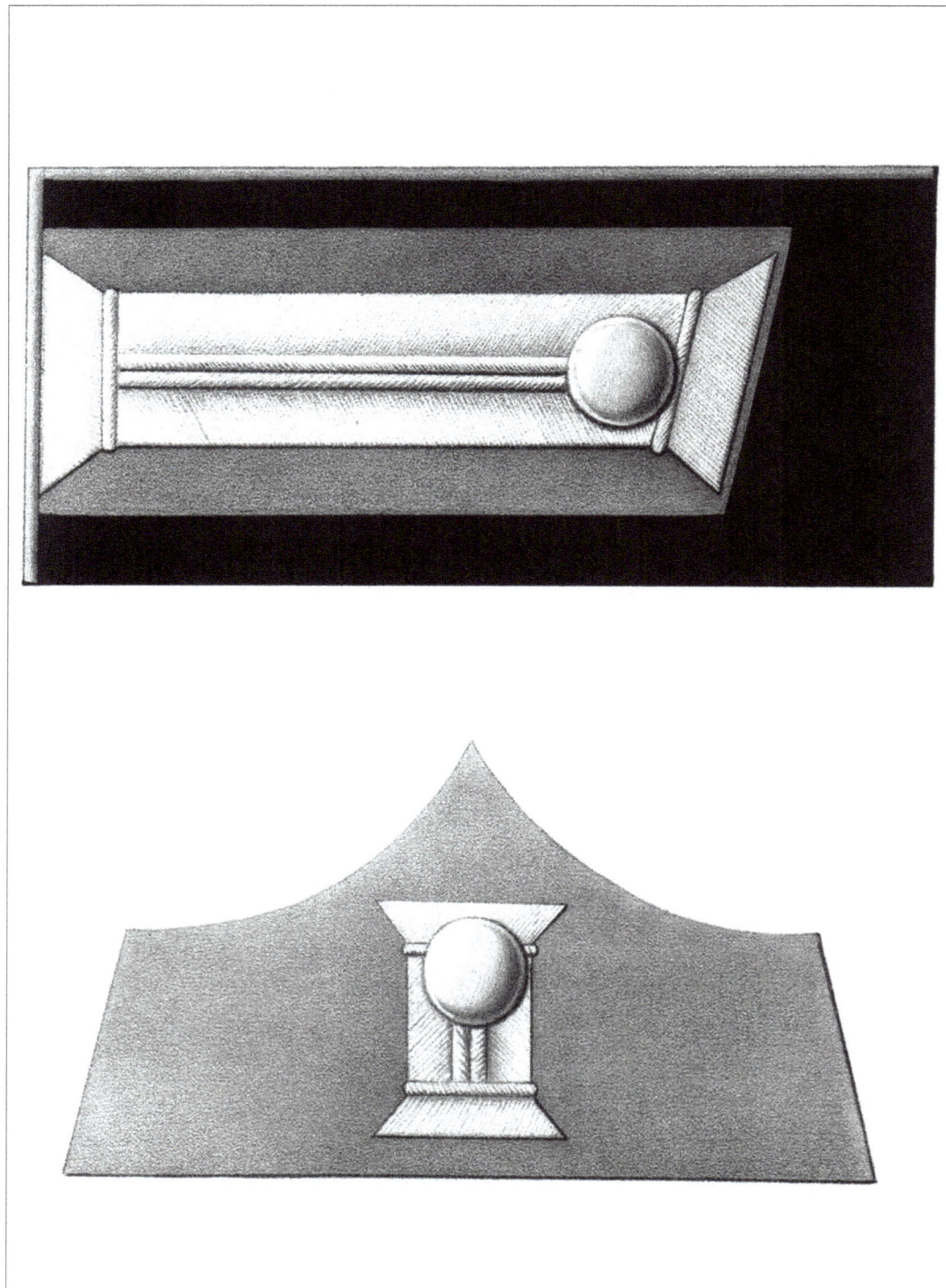

Embroidery on officers' coats in the L.-Gds. Horse-Jäger Regiment, since 18

2047b

Field-Grade Officer and Company-Grade Officers. L.-Gds. Horse-Jäger Regiment, 1816-1819

2048

Company-Grade Officer. L.-Gds. Horse-Jäger Regiment, 1817-1819

2049

Company-Grade Officer. L.-Gds. Horse-Jäger Regiment, 1817-1819

2050

Trumpeter and Private. L.-Gds. Horse-Jäger Regiment, 1817-1819

86

2051

Trumpeter. L.-Gds. Horse-Jäger Regiment, 1820-1825

Field-Grade Officer and Private. L.-Gds. Horse-Jäger Regiment, 1823-1825

2053

Non-Commissioned Officer and Company-Grade Officer. L.-Gds. Horse-Jäger Regiment, 1825

SOLDIERS, WEAPONS & UNIFORMS ALREADY PUBLISHED
(SOME TITLES)

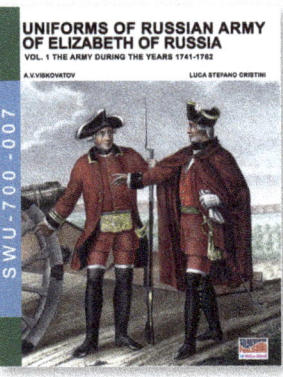
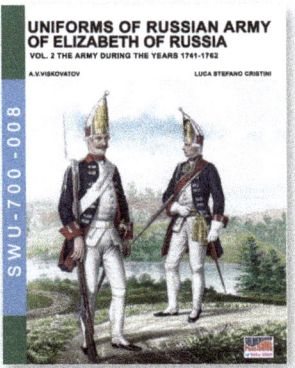

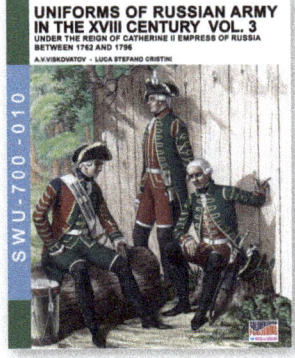

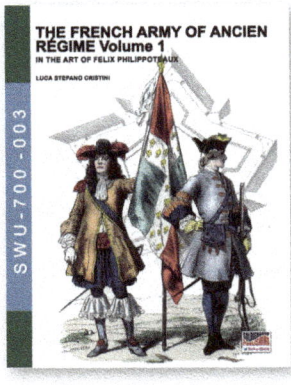
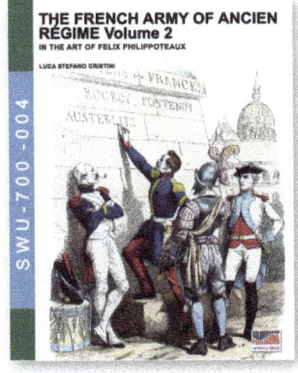

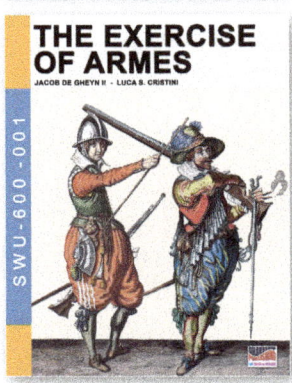

www.ingramcontent.com/pod-product-compliance
Lightning Source LLC
Chambersburg PA
CBHW041149120626
46547CB00020B/3160